The Blue Lace Curtain

I Talk You Talk Press

Old Secrets - Modern Mysteries Series Book 1

Copyright © 2018 I Talk You Talk Press

ISBN: 978-4-909733-15-3

www.italkyoutalk.com

info@italkyoutalk.com

All rights reserved. No part of this publication may be resold, reproduced, stored in retrieval system, copied in any form or by any means, electronic, mechanical, photocopying, recording or otherwise transmitted without the prior written permission from the publisher. You must not circulate this publication in any format, online or otherwise.

This is a work of fiction. Names, characters, businesses, organizations, products, places, events and incidents are either the products of the author's imagination or are used in a fictitious manner. We have no affiliation with any existing companies mentioned in this story. Any resemblance to actual persons, living or dead, existing stories or actual events is purely coincidental.

Although the author and publisher have made every effort to ensure that the contents of this book were correct at press time, the author and publisher do not assume and hereby disclaim any liability to any party for any loss, damage, or disruption caused by errors or omissions, whether such errors or omissions result from negligence, accident, or any other cause.

For more information, see the Copyright Notice on our website.

Image copyright: © MI.TI. #48214535 Standard License

CONTENTS

1. Why Andy went to Italy   1
2. Hotel guests in winter   3
3. Something strange   6
4. What James thought   9
5. Andy and James take a trip   12
6. Back at Hotel Peschi   15
7. At the theatre   19
8. Virginia explains   22
9. James investigates   26
10. Next morning   29
11. The plan   34
12. The rescue   39
13. Ned's story   45

I Talk You Talk Press

Thank You	50
About the Author	51

1. WHY ANDY WENT TO ITALY

Andy Fairweather was a research student. He lived in Birmingham, England, and went to the university. He was doing a doctorate degree on religion in the 11th century in Europe. He was clever, and he knew a lot about his subject.

The problem was that Andy was lazy. His professor was often angry with him. He had been working on his doctorate degree for four years. It was not finished. Finally his professor said, "If you do not finish writing your thesis by the end of March next year, I will give up. You will have to find another professor."

His parents said, "You don't have a job because you say you must finish writing your thesis. You live with us because you say you have no money. We give you money. Then you go out drinking and get up late. We don't want to give you any more money. You must get a job."

Andy sent an email to his uncle. He explained he was in trouble. Andy's uncle was a diplomat. His name was James. He was Andy's mother's brother. He lived in Rome. He was not married, and he was always very kind to Andy.

James sent a reply to Andy.

---*I do not think you will finish your thesis if you stay in England. You have too many friends. You go to too many parties. Why don't you come to Italy? I will find you somewhere quiet to stay. You can work ten hours a day and finish your thesis.*---

Andy thought this was a good idea. Andy's professor thought it was a good idea too. James paid for Andy to travel to Rome. Andy thought he would stay with his Uncle James in his beautiful apartment near the Spanish Steps, but James had a different idea.

"You need somewhere quiet. If you stay here, you will go out too much. I have friends who have a small hotel in the hills outside Florence. The hotel is very busy in spring and summer, but in winter there are usually no guests. I have arranged for you to live there."

"But Uncle James," said Andy. "I am sure I can work very well here. I can go to the library. I can study more Italian."

James can be very kind, but he can be tough too.

"Andy, if you want me to help you, if you want me to pay for you, you will do it my way. You will go to Hotel Peschi."

Andy went to Hotel Peschi. But he asked his Uncle James if he could visit him in Rome, one weekend a month. "I think I will be lonely in that hotel. Please let me come for a weekend every month."

James agreed.

2. HOTEL GUESTS IN WINTER

Hotel Peschi was very small. It was very busy during the fishing season because there was good fishing in the Sieve River. Fishing was not allowed between October and April, so there were usually no guests during those months.

Andy enjoyed staying at the hotel. The family was very nice. Their family name was Manetti. Signora Manetti did most of the cooking. Signor Manetti spoke some English. He had another fishermen's hotel in Abruzzo. His eldest son was the manager. Signor Manetti was always checking on him.

There was also a very pretty young woman who worked in the hotel. Her name was Luisa. Andy practiced speaking Italian with the Manetti family, and Luisa practiced English with Andy. Andy also worked on his thesis. He didn't work ten hours a day, but most days he worked for about six hours. By February, Andy had almost finished writing his thesis. This was good, because Andy had to give his thesis to his professor in England by the end of March.

Andy liked to sleep with the curtain of his bedroom open. When the sun came up, the light came through the window. It woke him up.

It was 7:00 am. He looked out of the window. Even though it was still winter, it was going to be a beautiful day. There was a small knock on the door. Andy smiled.

Some mornings, when Signora Manetti was not there, Luisa would bring Andy a cup of coffee. She would sit on Andy's bed and practice speaking English with him. Andy enjoyed Luisa's company very much.

Luisa came into the room, but this time she didn't have a cup of coffee for Andy. She said, "Andy, get up! Get up! There are guests. They arrived late last night. You know Signor Manetti went to Abruzzo yesterday. Signora Manetti went too. So you must come and talk to them!"

"Why me? Can't it wait? Come on, sit down and talk to me," said Andy.

"No, no. They are two American ladies. They are old. I have to make breakfast. I don't know what they want to eat. "

Andy was not happy. Luisa would not sit and chat with him. She wanted him to get out of bed and talk to two old ladies.

"All right! I'll come."

Andy got up, showered and got dressed. Even though it was quite cold, the two women were sitting at a table on the terrace. He went to talk to them.

"Good morning. I am Andy Fairweather. I am staying at this hotel. Can I help you?"

The women smiled at him. They were about sixty years old. One was blonde. She was wearing a lot of jewellery. Her clothes were very bright. She had a red Prada bag on her shoulder. The other woman had white hair. She was dressed very simply in a grey wool skirt and a thick grey jacket.

A rich woman and her companion, thought Andy.

The blonde woman spoke. "I am Elizabeth Schumacher from Chicago. This is my friend Jane Goodwell. She's from Scotland."

"Nice to meet you," said Andy. They shook hands.

"Can I help you?" asked Andy. "Luisa, who works here, wants to know what you want for breakfast."

"Is there a menu?' asked Elizabeth.

"In busy seasons, yes. But the hotel is almost empty at this time of year. I don't know why Luisa said you could stay."

"She's a very kind young woman," answered Elizabeth. "We arrived very late. We were tired and we asked if we could stay. What do you usually have for breakfast?"

"Coffee and bread," said Andy.

"That will be fine for me. How about you, Jane?"

The white haired woman nodded.

"OK. I will tell Luisa."

Andy went to the kitchen to tell Luisa.

"Thank you," said Luisa. "Now you go and sit on the terrace near them. I will bring breakfast for everyone."

Andy went back to his room. He picked up a book to read. He was still angry. Luisa had not brought coffee to his bedroom, and he had got up earlier than he wanted. He didn't want to talk to the two women.

Andy sat on the terrace. He sat at a table far away from Elizabeth and Jane. He read his book.

When Elizabeth and Jane finished their breakfast, they came over to Andy's table.

"Thank you for your help," said Elizabeth.

"You're welcome," said Andy. "Where are you planning to go today?"

"Oh, we think we will have a quiet day. Maybe take a walk."

"You are not leaving? I thought you must have got lost last night." Andy was surprised.

"We like it here. It is very quiet and beautiful. We think we will stay for a few days."

The two women smiled at Andy and walked away.

Andy was very annoyed. Signora Manetti was away. He could have had a few days alone with Luisa. She would have cooked all Andy's favourite meals and they would have drunk wine together in the evenings.

Now that the two women were staying at Hotel Peschi, Luisa would not do any of those things. She would work hard. She would tell him to interpret. It was not a good day.

3. SOMETHING STRANGE

Three days later, the women were still staying at Hotel Peschi. Signor and Signora Manetti were still in Abruzzo, because the fishing season started a month earlier there. Luisa said Senor Manetti was helping his son prepare for all the guests who would start arriving in March. Luisa was very busy. She had no time for Andy. She would not serve Andy meals in his room. She always said, "You go and sit in the dining room. Be nice to the other guests. I am too busy to do anything special for you."

Andy always sat as far away from the women as he could. But now he was a little more interested in them. At first he thought the white haired woman, Jane, was an employee of Elizabeth's. But he noticed that her clothes were very expensive. She didn't wear a lot of jewellery, but what she did wear was very good. The two women shared a bedroom. Andy thought that was strange. *I am sure they have a lot of money. Why share a room?*

Elizabeth carried the red Prada bag with her everywhere. The women had a rental car. It was parked in front of the hotel. But they never went anywhere. They took walks near the hotel, but mostly they stayed indoors, or on the terrace. The white-haired woman read a lot. She was very quiet. She didn't speak much. Elizabeth seemed nervous. She didn't read so much. She looked at her mobile phone all the time, and sent many text messages. She walked up and down the terrace even when it was cold.

On the fourth morning, Andy got up early. He looked at his books and notes on the table in his room. He looked at his computer.

Vacation today! he thought.

He found Luisa in the kitchen. He sat at the table and drank a cup of coffee with her. Then he said, "I'm going out for the day."

"But you have to talk to the guests," said Luisa.

"Talk to them yourself," said Andy. "English practice!"

Andy walked to Dicomano and caught the bus to Rufina. He planned to see his friend Antonio. Antonio was the son of the local garage owner. He was pleased to see Andy.

"Shall we sit in the plaza and watch the girls?" he asked.

"Good idea. And let's drink some wine," answered Andy.

Andy and Antonio enjoyed watching the girls in the plaza. Then they went to Antonio's home for lunch. Andy drank a lot of wine. Then it was time for Andy to leave. The last bus from Rufina to Dicomano was at 3:00pm.

When Andy got off the bus in Dicomano, the town was empty. It is a long walk from Dicomano to Hotel Peschi, and it is uphill. Usually Andy was lucky, and a car or van would come up the road. Then the driver would stop and give him a ride.

On this day Andy was not lucky. He was rather drunk and he became very tired. He stopped often to have a rest. Finally, he could see Hotel Peschi. It was about 500m away.

I'll have one more rest, thought Andy.

He walked off the road and found a patch of grass under a tree. The tree was on the edge of a path that went from Hotel Peschi to the Sieve River. Andy was wondering whether the path might be quicker than the road, when he heard voices. It was Elizabeth and Jane. He didn't want to talk to them. He moved quickly and stood behind a tall tree. The two women were walking down the path. He listened. First he was surprised because Jane was talking a lot.

"Virginia. You have to calm down! I am sure it will be OK."

Andy was sure it was Jane's voice. But who was Virginia?

"Oh Sarah, I hope you're right. But it's been four days now, and they haven't contacted me."

Andy knew that was Elizabeth talking.

"They will. They know where we are. If they want the dagger, they will have to contact you."

"When?" Elizabeth sounded very stressed. "When I think of my poor Ned, stuck up there behind that blue lace curtain! I wish I could go and see him."

"I know you do, but we agreed. It's too dangerous for him. These people might be watching us. They know where we are. There's only one road from Hotel Peschi. It would be easy for them to watch the road and follow us."

The two women disappeared down the path. Andy could hear their voices, but he couldn't hear what they were saying.

Andy was very puzzled. The white-haired woman had talked a lot, but she was usually so quiet. It seemed her name was Sarah. It seemed Elizabeth's name was really Virginia. *Who were these women, and what were they doing?*

Andy went back to the road and walked up to the hotel. He didn't want to meet the women on the path. At the hotel, he went to see Luisa.

"Luisa," he said. "When Elizabeth and Jane came, did you take their passports?"

"No, I didn't," said Luisa. "Is it a problem? I know Signor Manetti asks for passports, but I don't know what he does with them. I thought it would be OK. Now I am worried. Do you think I should have asked for them?"

"Don't worry," said Andy. "But do you have their credit card? How will they pay for the hotel?"

"On the first night they gave me money for one night and breakfast. The next day, they gave me money for three days; three meals a day, and a room for two people. This morning the white-haired woman gave me the same amount of money again."

Andy went to his room. He lay down on his bed. He tried to remember everything he had heard. But he was still a little drunk and he was very tired. He fell asleep.

4. WHAT JAMES THOUGHT

The next morning, the two women were in the dining room as usual. Nothing seemed to have changed. Andy watched them.

Who were they, and why were they at Hotel Peschi?

Andy did not have much time to think. Today was Friday, and he was travelling to Rome for the weekend.

He was not lonely at Hotel Peschi, and life was now quite interesting.

Maybe I should stay here this weekend, he thought. But his uncle was expecting him. Also, his uncle might take him to an expensive restaurant. Andy packed a bag and walked down the hill to Dicomano. He had a bus and two trains to catch. It would take about five hours to get to Rome.

It was late afternoon when Andy arrived at his uncle's apartment. Rosita, the housekeeper, opened the door. She gave him coffee, and said his uncle would return from work at about 7:00pm. Andy had a shower. Then he went out to sit on the Spanish Steps to watch people. At 6:30pm he went back. The housekeeper was getting ready to go home.

"Do you know if we will eat here tonight, or in a restaurant?" Andy asked Rosita.

"Signor James asked me to buy food for tonight. He plans to cook for you. You are lucky. He is a very good cook," answered the housekeeper. "I have bought extra food for breakfasts. I do not come again until Monday morning. I think tomorrow you will go to a restaurant. Please enjoy your weekend."

The meal was delicious. Fettuccine with a creamy mushroom sauce, followed by lamb chops cooked with lemon, garlic and rosemary. Rosita was right. James was a very good cook. While they were eating, Andy and James talked about sport and politics, and shared family gossip. After the meal, they sat in James' study. James brought in a plate of cheese and fruit that Rosita had prepared.

Even with the central hearing on, it was getting cold. So James lit the fire, and they sat and drank the last of the bottle of wine.

"How is everything at Hotel Peschi?" asked James. "How is your thesis?"

"My thesis is OK. I think I can finish next month," answered Andy. "But I am enjoying a little mystery at Hotel Peschi right now."

"Oh really? What's that?" James smiled.

Andy explained about the Manetti's trip to Abruzzo, about the two surprise guests and the mystery of the women's names.

James laughed. "I think you should be working on your thesis and not playing detective! I am sure there is a very simple reason. Maybe you didn't hear well. You said you went to see Antonio Perugia in Rufina. I don't know him, but I remember his father. Every time I visited Alberto Perugia I drank a lot of wine. Maybe you were drunk."

Andy laughed too. "I did drink a lot with Antonio that day. Yes, I am sure you're right. There's no mystery. Just my mistake."

Andy was quiet for a minute. He looked at his uncle. James had opened another bottle of wine, and he was pouring it.

"But you know," Andy said slowly. "The blonde American woman seemed very worried. She was talking about someone called Ned. I wonder who he is? He's in danger and he's behind a blue lace curtain."

There was a crash as James dropped the wine bottle. Wine was spilt all over the table and the carpet.

Andy went to the kitchen to get a cloth to clean up. When he came back, James was standing by the window. He had opened the curtain. He was looking at the street.

"You didn't say anything about a blue lace curtain," said James.

"No. It was just one of the things the American woman said."

James turned around. "Can you clean up here? I will make coffee. I need to talk to you."

For the next hour, James asked Andy questions. What did the

women look like, what did they wear, and even what jewellery could he remember. James asked again and again for Andy to repeat the words he had heard.

Finally Andy said, "Uncle James, I'm sorry. I can't remember anything else. And I don't understand why it is important."

"Sorry," said James. "It was those words, 'the blue lace curtain'. When I was young, about your age, I heard a young woman describe a blue lace curtain. It was a long time ago, but I was wondering if it is the same person."

Andy looked at his uncle. "And now, what do you think?"

"I think it is the same person," said James.

"You were very surprised. It seems to be serious. Are there ghosts from the past that will cause you trouble?" asked Andy.

James smiled. "I am not sure if this is a ghost or an angel."

"So, long ago, you knew one of the women at Hotel Peschi. Which one? It must be the blonde American woman. She is the one who said 'blue lace curtain'."

James was quiet for a long time. Then he said, "Maybe I knew both women. I can't be sure. But I think so. If I am right, they stayed at Hotel Peschi many years ago. Signor Manetti was a young man then, but I am sure he would remember them."

"Why did they pretend it was the first time to visit the hotel? It's bad luck for them that Signor Manetti is not there, especially since he is away for so much longer than usual."

"I am not sure that it is bad luck," said James slowly. "Why don't you go to bed? You must be tired. I think I will make some phone calls.".

5. ANDY AND JAMES TAKE A TRIP

The next morning, James woke Andy at 8.00am.

"Come on. Get up! I was making phone calls until very late last night, and now we have a lot to do. Get dressed and pack your bag. There is coffee and bread in the kitchen."

Andy got out of bed. His uncle seemed very cheerful this morning. *What is he planning?* Andy wondered.

During an earlier weekend in Rome, he and his uncle had stayed a night at a villa in the country. Perhaps James had planned something similar.

Andy was drinking his second cup of coffee when his uncle appeared in the kitchen.

"I suppose you didn't bring a suit with you? How about at Hotel Peschi?"

Andy shook his head, "I have a good jacket and a tie, but no suit."

"Never mind. I'll lend you one of mine. I'd better get it now." James went out of the room. Andy was still wondering what was going to happen.

When James came back, he sat down at the table and poured himself a coffee.

"We're driving to Florence today. And I want you to go back up to the hotel."

"But!" Andy choked on the last of his coffee.

"Just listen," said James.

"I want you to invite the two women to a concert. It's tonight. Bel canto at the Pergola Theatre. I've arranged the tickets, and we'll pick them up on the way. I reserved a box. I thought that would be best."

"James," Andy spoke loudly. "Why are you doing this?"

James looked at his coffee cup. He didn't reply.

Why was he doing this? he asked himself. In his head, he heard a voice from almost forty years ago,

---Hi James! I'm calling from the post office in Dicomano. Virginia and I love Hotel Peschi. Thanks to you, they're looking after us like daughters. We're spending a lot of time at Premilcuore with Victor. His house is amazing. It has a tower, like a lighthouse. There's only one small room on each floor. I want you to see it. The tower has one window, quite high up. And it looks so strange because it's got a blue lace curtain. I've never seen a curtain like it! Please come. Victor is so in love with Virginia. He doesn't say anything. He just stares at her. I wish he would get some courage and ask her to marry him. I'm sure she'll say no, though. Anyway with those two, it's a bit lonely…..---

"James!"

James came back from his memories. Andy was staring at him.

"Are you OK? You looked like your mind was miles away."

James drank a large mouthful of coffee. "Yes, I'm OK, just remembering."

"What is it about this blue lace curtain?" asked Andy. "And why do you want me to invite these two women to a concert?"

"When I was studying French and Spanish at the Sorbonne, there were many other international students there. I made a lot of friends. Two of my friends were called Virginia and Sarah. They shared an apartment. The summer I was finishing my research, Virginia and Sarah went on vacation to Italy. I already knew the Manettis. Your grandfather was very keen on fly-fishing, and we used to stay at Hotel Peschi every year. I arranged for them to stay there. There was another student, a bit older. He was from Bulgaria, but his grandmother was Italian. He had a house in Premilcuore. You know where that is? Well, the house had a blue lace curtain. There are too many coincidences. That's why I think I know these women. You told me that the women at the hotel, who are calling themselves Elizabeth and Jane, are really Virginia and Sarah. So I think they are the same Virginia and Sarah that I used to know."

"Why don't you just call them?" asked Andy. "This all seems very complicated."

"I can't just call them because they are not using their real names. If I call, they will know that someone has discovered their real names. You told me about their conversation in the woods. They are worried or frightened about something. You told me they talked about a dagger and maybe a kidnapping. I want to help them if I can, but I need to find out more. Too many people who live around Dicomano know me, so I don't want to go there. They have long memories in the country. They might connect Virginia and Sarah to me. Your job is to get them to Florence. Even after forty years, I am sure I will recognize them."

Andy sighed. "OK. Are you taking your Alfa Romeo?"

"Of course," answered James.

"Great. Can I drive?"

6. BACK AT HOTEL PESCHI

James dropped Andy in Rufina, on the opposite side of the town from Alberto Perugia's garage. Andy was starting to wonder about his uncle. He seemed to have some undercover skills. *Was that normal for a diplomat?*

Andy took the bus to Dicomano. He was lucky, because the postman stopped and gave him a ride up the hill to the hotel. The hotel was very quiet. He could hear Luisa in the kitchen. He walked past the kitchen very quietly and out onto the terrace. The two women were sitting at a table at the far end. Sarah was reading as usual.

I must remember to think of her as Jane, thought Andy.

Elizabeth was staring down at the road that curved down the hill to Dicomano. As usual, she seemed tense. It looked like she was waiting for something.

Andy walked over and sat at their table. Jane put down her book and smiled at him.

"I went to Rome to visit my uncle, but he was very busy. So I couldn't stay. He gave me three tickets for a concert in Florence as an apology. Would you ladies do me the honour of coming to the concert with me?"

"Thank you," smiled Jane. "But you know, we came here for a quiet time. We are really not interested in going out, especially not as far as Florence."

"Oh, please. It's only about forty-five minutes by car. I have ordered a chauffeured car to take us. I hate going to the theatre alone."

Jane was firm. "I'm really sorry, but we can't go."

Andy panicked. He had to persuade them somehow. "There will be someone special there. He wants to meet you."

Elizabeth had been staring down the road, but now, she turned around and gasped.

"A meeting?"

"Oh, just someone who would like to see you." Andy was embarrassed.

Elizabeth's face went very white. She was holding Jane's hand tightly.

"Can we talk about it please?" asked Jane. "When do you need to know if we will go or not?"

"Oh, well it's four o'clock now, and the car is coming at six o'clock," answered Andy. He felt very uncomfortable. Elizabeth looked like a statue, and even Jane, who was always so calm, looked worried.

"I'll leave you to think about it," said Andy and left the terrace.

However, he didn't go to his room. He ran down the stairs and into a storage room. The storage room had a window directly under the terrace. He dragged an empty wine box over to the window and stood on it. The window had not been opened for a long time. It was stiff, and he couldn't risk making any noise. Finally, he got it open, and put his head out of the window. Elizabeth and Jane were directly above him. He could hear them talking.

"But Sarah, this must be it! They said they would contact us here. And they have!"

"But Virginia, we thought it would be a phone call. You know, 'drop the item in this telephone box and we will release him'; like a kidnapping ransom. This seems too complicated. And Andy doesn't seem the kind of messenger they would use."

"How do we know who they would use? They're clever you know! It might be our only chance! We have to go!"

"But don't you see? It might be a trap. They could just drive us away. Then they'd have the dagger, and who knows what would happen to Ned, or to us? It's too risky!"

"Sarah, please!"

"Let me think…"

The two women must have moved away from the edge of the

terrace, because Andy couldn't hear their voices anymore. He went to his room and lay on the bed. After a few minutes there was a knock on the door. It was Jane.

"I'm sorry. You must think we are very ungrateful. We were just surprised. We would like to go to the concert very much. We're also very interested in your friend who wants to meet us. Who is it?"

"Oh, just someone I met." Andy hoped he was not making the situation worse.

"Is he Italian? We don't know many Italians."

"No, he's English."

"Oh." Jane looked puzzled. "OK. Never mind. Just one thing though. It was very kind of you to order a car. But we think we would rather meet you at the theatre. We'll leave a little earlier than six. I have some things I want to do on the way. So if you can give us our tickets, we can meet you there."

"Great!" said Andy, although he thought this was not great at all. He gave Jane two of the tickets. "The concert's at the Pergola Theatre. We have a box. I'll see you there around seven?"

"I'm looking forward to it," Jane smiled and went away with the tickets.

Andy called James. "They think it's a trap! It seems to be all about kidnapping and ransoms. They'll go to the theatre, but in their own car. What should I do?"

"Calm down," said James. "This sounds serious, and now it is much more difficult to make sure they are safe. Never mind. You go in the car and meet them at the theatre."

Andy took a shower and dressed in the borrowed suit. He heard the women's car leave, but he waited in his room. It was still only 5:15. Luisa ran into his room.

"The foreign ladies have gone out! They said they would not want a meal tonight. They said you are going to take them to a concert in Florence! My God! Why them? Do you think because I work in a hotel I cannot be taken to a concert? I hate you!"

Andy put his head in his hands. "Luisa! It's not like that. Believe me. I don't want to take these women to the theatre. But I have to. Please calm down!"

Luisa ran out of the room and slammed the door. Everything on the desk and dressing table shook.

Andy put a book in his pocket and walked outside. He could hear

Luisa banging pots in the kitchen.

Oh, well, thought Andy. *Perhaps she won't ask me to look after these women any more. And maybe it means she likes me as more than a friend!*

7. AT THE THEATRE

The driver stopped outside the Pergola Theatre in Florence. Andy took the driver's mobile phone number.

"I'll call you when we want to be collected," he told the driver.

Andy went inside the theatre. It was very old and beautiful. He showed his ticket to an usher, and she led him up a narrow stairway to a corridor. There was a row of doors on the left. These were the doors to the boxes. The usher was very pretty. Andy thought she looked like Luisa. He hoped Luisa would forgive him. She was very angry, but perhaps Andy could explain that it was his uncle's fault.

The usher stopped outside a door and smiled. Andy went in. There was a row of six seats. On one side there was a table with an ice bucket. There was a bottle of champagne in the bucket, and four champagne glasses next to the bucket. James was sitting in one of the seats. He saw Andy look at the champagne.

"I don't know if it is a good idea," said James. He seemed nervous.

"Champagne is always a good idea," said Andy cheerfully. Andy loved champagne.

The two men sat and waited. There were 30 minutes to wait until the concert began. Andy tried to tell James about Luisa, and how angry she was. James didn't listen. James didn't talk at all. He sat staring over the little balcony at the front of the box. People were arriving and sitting down, ready for the concert.

The door of the box opened. James rushed to the corner of the box behind the door. Andy jumped up.

Elizabeth and Jane walked in. "Did you find a car park?" asked

Andy. He was wondering why James was hiding behind the door.

"Yes, thank you," said Jane. Elizabeth and Jane were looking around the box. They seemed puzzled. Elizabeth was holding the red Prada bag in two hands.

Jane shut the door and James stepped forward. He was smiling.

"Sarah! Virginia! Or should I call you Jane and Elizabeth? It's wonderful to see you after so many years! You really haven't changed at all."

Sarah's face went white. She looked like a statue. Virginia looked at James.

"You! You are working with them. What kind of monster are you?" she shouted.

"What?" James looked stunned.

Andy put his hand on Sarah's arm and led her to a seat. She sat down. She was looking at James as though he were a ghost.

Virginia was still shouting. "How could you? My poor Ned! You are an evil man. I never thought it would be someone I used to know!"

"Who's Ned?" asked James. He was talking to Virginia, but he was staring at Sarah.

Virginia threw the red handbag at James. "There you are! You've got what you wanted! Now let Ned go!"

Virginia was making a lot of noise. People in the theatre were staring up at them. Some people were standing so that they could see what was happening.

Andy was getting nervous. "I think we should leave," he said. "They will be sending the manager soon."

"I knew it," shouted Virginia. "Sarah was right! It's a trap!"

"No!" said James loudly. "I came here to help you. Calm down!"

Virginia looked at James. She sat down and started to cry. "I don't believe you!"

"Come on, everyone," said Andy. "Let's talk outside."

He picked up the red handbag and gave it to Virginia. Sarah stood up. She took Virginia's arm. "Come on," she said. "I don't know what is going on, but these are not the people we wanted to meet."

She took Virginia out through the door. James followed them. Andy stopped to pick up the bottle of champagne. It hadn't been opened and it seemed a pity to waste it.

They went down the stairs and outside. They stood on the

pavement outside the theatre. People were still going into the theatre for the concert.

Virginia was crying. Sarah was holding her.

"Listen," said James. "I understand you came to the theatre to meet someone. I understand you are in trouble. I know you don't want to talk to me. But I can help you. I want to help you. Please come somewhere where we can talk."

He looked at Sarah. She nodded. "Virginia," she said. "This is all wrong. But I think we do need help now. Please listen to what he has to say. I want to know what James is doing here. Ned might be in more danger now. I think that is James' fault. So he should help us."

Virginia just cried. Sarah sighed. "We will come with you, but I hope you have a good story."

Andy took out his mobile phone and called the driver. The driver was very surprised. "But Senor! You said after the concert. It has only been 30 minutes! Don't you like bel canto?"

"I don't know," answered Andy. "I have no idea what it is. But there is a change of plan. Please come now."

The driver came quickly and Sarah, Virginia, James and Andy got into the car.

"Where to?" asked the driver.

"We will go to my hotel," said James. "I think that is the best place."

He gave the hotel name to the driver. He told the driver to wait outside the hotel.

8. VIRGINIA EXPLAINS

James' room at the hotel was a suite. Andy thought it was wonderful. Two rooms filled with flowers. A table with drinks. Andy was thirsty. He went over to the drinks table.

"What would you like to drink?" he asked.

No one answered him. Andy poured two glasses of sherry and two whiskies. Sarah and Virginia were sitting on a sofa. James was standing by the window.

Andy gave everyone a drink. He drank his whisky very quickly, and poured another one for himself.

Andy sat down and looked at Virginia. She started talking.

"I don't think you will understand what has happened, unless I explain about Ned. He's my husband. I met him in Washington DC, about three years after I left Paris. It was at a party at the Smithsonian Museum. I was working for a congressman. The people I worked with were all very clever and very ambitious. It was exciting and I loved the life. But I got very tired. I wanted something different. I wanted to change my life. Then I met Ned. He is not very good looking and he is not very clever, but he is a very kind man. I fell in love with him because he was so different from the other men I knew.

"He is an archaeologist. Not a very good one. He got a job at a small university in the Midwest United States. It didn't pay very well, and he never got promoted. But it didn't matter. I had enough money for both of us. My grandmother, and then my father died, and they left me a lot of money.

"Also, you remember our old friend Victor from our university days? Well, I stayed in touch with him. He never married. We used to visit him sometimes here in Italy. When he died about three years ago, he left me all his money and the house in Premilcuore. I was so surprised. Ned was not happy about this. I think he thought Victor and I were lovers. We weren't then. At least not after I met Ned. Long ago, we were lovers. When Sarah and I stayed at Hotel Peschi that summer, we were lovers then. Victor wanted to marry me, but I said no. I went back to America. That was the end of it. But I don't think Ned believed me. I think he was jealous.

"We live near the university. We have two sons. They are not like their father. They are both clever and very successful. The trouble started when our sons left home and went to university. Adam, our younger son, studied physics. He did very well, and now he is a professor at Harvard. Our older son Mark studied law, and after a short time working for a law firm, he went into politics. I got bored because our sons were not at home. So I started travelling more. I went on trips abroad. I went to New York and San Francisco to shop and go to the opera. I made new friends, and I was often away from home. I helped Mark too. I used my money to help him get elected as a congressman. I suddenly enjoyed politics again.

"Poor Ned was left at home. He was lonely, and I think he felt bad. He felt that he was not successful and that I didn't love him anymore. This wasn't true. I love Ned a lot, but I was always away. When I was home, I only talked about Mark and Adam. So I think what happened was my fault.

"Early this year Ned retired. He thought we would do things together. Travel, work in the garden, read books....things like that. He was asked to help with an archaeological trip for students to Petra, in Jordan. He asked me to go with him. I should have gone with him. But Mark had a chance to be selected as the chairman of an important congressional committee. I was so excited. I told Ned to go alone. I was too busy and I wanted to stay home.

"So he went to Jordan without me. He took the students. He sent emails every day, and I thought he was happy. He is not a very good archaeologist, but he knows a lot. Students like him too. He is very kind and patient.

"Then I got a strange email. He said he was about to make a great discovery. It would make him famous. He was excited. He said I would be very proud of him.

"Then there were no more emails. I emailed him, but he never answered. I was worried. I telephoned the university. They talked to the trip leader in Petra, who said that Ned had left the student group and gone somewhere alone. The university people were not worried. They said he told them he had some private work to do for a few days.

"Then a parcel arrived. It had been posted in Florence. It was old T-shirts and socks and paperback books, but inside was a dagger. There was no letter. But the T-shirts were Ned's.

"The next day, two men came to see me. They were Americans. They said they knew I had got a parcel from Ned. They knew about the dagger. They wanted it. I told them I didn't know what they were talking about.

"Then they said that Ned was their prisoner, and they wouldn't let him go until they got the dagger. They said they would come back. I was very worried and frightened.

"I called my son, Mark. I told him everything, and asked him what to do. He was very angry. He said, 'What has the stupid fool done?' He shouldn't talk about his father like that. I was upset.

"He said I couldn't go to the police. If I went to the police, the story would be in the newspapers. That would be very bad for Mark and his political future. If there were any stories about his father being connected with criminals or gangs or terrorists, he would have no chance of becoming committee chairman.

"Then he said that if Ned had got into trouble, he would have to get himself out of trouble. He made me promise not to go to the police. He said he was busy and hung up. I was so angry with Mark. I thought he was so selfish.

"About two hours later, Mark called back. He said that after we finished our call, he started to worry. He called a friend in the police. After that, the FBI called Mark. They were asking questions about Ned. Mark told me I might be in danger. I must not talk to anyone. I must not use the telephone. He told me to take a trip somewhere. Visit some friends, perhaps. He said he would send one of his staff to pick up the dagger. He would find his father. He would fix everything. He told me not to worry. But that night Sarah called me."

Virginia stopped talking. She looked at Sarah.

Sarah said, "I'll explain the next bit. I live in Scotland. I was tidying up the garden when the telephone rang. It was Ned. He said it was too dangerous to call Virginia. He wanted to keep her safe. He said he had done something very stupid, and now he was in a lot of trouble. People were looking for him. He was hiding in Florence, but he thought they would find him. He had another place to hide, and was going there."

James interrupted. "Who were 'they'?"

"He didn't say. He just said, 'Tell Virginia the blue lace curtain, she will know'. He sounded very frightened. He said, 'I'll have to go. Promise me you will help Virginia,' and he rang off."

"I called Virginia but she wouldn't talk to me. I tried to tell her about Ned's telephone call. She just asked if she could come and stay with me in Scotland.

"Virginia arrived the following night. She was exhausted and went to bed. She had brought the dagger with her.

"Someone must have got Ned's mobile phone, because while she was sleeping, I got a phone call from Italy. The man told me that Virginia must take the dagger to Florence. I didn't understand what he was talking about. The man gave me a phone number. He said Virginia must not use her real name. He told me she must call the number and tell him where she was staying. They would contact her, and they would take the dagger. Then Ned would be free. He said if she didn't do it, they would kill Ned.

"So Virginia and I came to Italy. We knew that Ned must be at Premilcuore in Victor's old house. In the house with the blue lace curtain. I called Senor Manetti at Hotel Peschi. He remembered us. I explained that we needed a place to stay, but that we would be using false names. That it might be dangerous. Dear Senor Manetti agreed to help us. He said he would take his wife and go to stay with his son. Then no one at the hotel would know us or remember us."

Virginia started to talk again. "I called the number and told the man that we were at Hotel Peschi. The man said he would contact us. So we have been waiting at the hotel. We thought that Andy must be a messenger. Then when I saw James at the theatre, I thought he must be the gang leader."

9. JAMES INVESTIGATES

James walked over to Virginia and held her hand. "Can you believe I had nothing to do with this?"

Virginia smiled. "Yes, I believe you. But I don't know how you found out about Sarah and me."

James smiled too. "Andy is my nephew. He heard you talking in the woods near Hotel Peschi. He realized you were not using your real names. He heard you say something about a blue lace curtain. I guessed it might be you and Sarah. I thought you must be in trouble. So I came here to help you."

Virginia was surprised. "You remembered about Victor's house and the strange tower with the curtain?"

James looked sad. "I remember everything from that last summer. I left the Sorbonne in October that year. That summer was very special to me."

Virginia looked at Sarah, but Sarah was looking down at her hands. She didn't say anything. But Virginia smiled. She looked as though she knew something.

"Now," said James. "We need a plan. First, why is this dagger so important?"

Virginia opened her red handbag and took out a box. She handed the box to James. He opened it and took out the dagger. It was slightly curved, and had beautiful jewels set in the handle. He looked at it carefully. "Ned sent this dagger to you. Where did he get it?"

"I think he must have found it in Petra. Or somewhere near Petra," said Virginia.

"I did some research on the Internet before we left Scotland," said Sarah. "I thought that the dagger would be Arabic, and very, very old. But it doesn't look like any of the pictures I found on Google."

"OK," answered James. "We don't know why it's important. And why did he take it to Italy? Why did Ned go to Italy?"

Andy spoke up. "Why is the FBI interested? Who were the men who went to Virginia's house?"

"We don't know very much, do we?" said James. "But I can find out what this dagger is. At least I think I can find out how old it is, and where it's from. It is not that old. Not as old as 5th or 6th century. I also know some people in Interpol and in the FBI. I will contact them. I will try to find out what happened. Andy must go to Premilcuore."

James turned to Andy.

"Andy I think you should ask Antonio Perugia to go with you. Then you can go on Antonio's motorbike. You must borrow some clothes from Antonio, and be sure to wear a bike helmet. Someone might be following Virginia and Sarah. They might have seen you. But if you are dressed like a young Italian man and are wearing a helmet, maybe no one will recognise you. In Premilcuore, you must find the house with the blue lace curtain and watch it. Please try to find out if there is anyone inside, and if anyone is watching the house. Be careful. It could be dangerous. I think you should leave now. The car we hired and the driver are still outside. Ask him to take you to Rufina. Tell him to stop outside a hotel. Don't let the driver see you going to Antonio's house."

Andy was pleased to have a job to do. It would be nice to go with Antonio. They always had fun. There might be a chance to watch girls, and drink. That reminded him of the champagne. He took the bottle and stood near the door holding it.

"James?" he said.

"Yes?"

"Do you think I could have some money? I'll have to pay the driver. And we'll have to pay for petrol and food and things."

James sighed. "I suppose you will need money."

He gave Andy some Euros. Then Andy left.

James called the hotel reception and reserved another room. He went into the bedroom of the suite and came out with his laptop computer and his travel bag.

"You can stay in this suite tonight," he said to Virginia and Sarah. "Lock the door and don't let anyone come in. If you have any trouble, call me." He gave Virginia a piece of paper. "Here's my mobile phone number. I'll be in room 1047. Can I take a photograph of the dagger?"

Virginia nodded. James photographed the dagger with his mobile phone. Then he went to the door. Standing at the door, he smiled at Virginia. "Sleep well and try not to worry!"

10. NEXT MORNING

James called the suite early the next morning. "I have ordered breakfast from room service. They will bring it to the suite soon. I will come now. Look through the spy hole in the door. Don't open the door unless you are sure it is me," he said.

When he came into the room he looked tired. Soon after, the room service waiter knocked on the door. James told Virginia and Sarah to go into the bedroom. He opened the door very carefully and took the cart with the food and drinks from the waiter. He didn't let the waiter come into the room.

Sarah and Virginia came out of the bedroom and arranged the food and drinks on the table. They were still wearing the clothes they had worn to the theatre. James sat down. Sarah poured a coffee for him.

"Thank you," he smiled at Sarah. "Well, the time difference between Europe and the United States was useful last night. I spent a lot of time sending emails and calling people, and I know some of what happened in Jordan."

Sarah and Virginia sat down and stared at him.

"So tell!" said Virginia.

"The first thing is that the dagger is not Arabic. It is Spanish, about 16th century. I sent the photograph to a friend of mine. Then he sent it to a colleague in a museum here in Italy. The colleague is sure that it is the dagger that many people believe once belonged to Cesare Borgia. It was stolen from a museum in Rome about three years ago."

James looked uncomfortable. "And Virginia, I'm sorry. It seems that the FBI doesn't believe Ned found the dagger. They think he stole it. They think he is a member of a gang that steals from museums and private collectors."

"Ned!" Virginia was amazed. "I think that Ned might do something stupid, especially if he wanted to impress his sons. I think if a dagger like that was lying about somewhere, or if someone offered to sell it to him, the temptation would be too much. But he's weak, not dishonest. Why do they think he is a member of a gang of thieves?"

"In this case, because he was in Italy at the time the dagger was stolen," James explained.

"Three years ago? Oh, yes. We came to Premilcuore to see Victor just before he died. But that doesn't mean anything!"

"I am confused," said Sarah. "How is a robbery in Italy connected to Petra?"

James held out his cup and Sarah poured him another coffee.

"This is what I was able to find out," he started. "I don't know much about Petra, but it seems that there is a lot of archaeological investigation. Tourists can't visit most of the areas being studied, but with special introductions and permits, it is possible to enter these zones. Ned got an introduction from someone in a Saudi Arabian university, and was allowed to go anywhere he wanted. He wasn't allowed to take the students with him, and he had a local guide with him at all times.

"There are many caves cut into the rocks. These haven't all been studied yet, but apparently that was where Ned always wanted to go. At some point he got the dagger. It seems it came from one of the caves. Whether Ned found it, or someone else found it and sold it to Ned, I don't know.

"About the time that Ned arrived in Jordan, Interpol found a connection between Ned's guide in Petra and a gang of museum thieves. So they asked the police in Jordan to watch the guide. Then, when Ned was exploring the caves with the guide, they checked up on Ned. They discovered that Ned had been in Italy when the dagger was stolen. They told the Jordanian police about this too, and so the police were also watching Ned.

"When Ned spent so much time looking at caves, the police thought there might be something interesting there. They started looking in the caves. Finally, they found one with some boxes in it, but they were empty. By that time, Ned and the guide had disappeared. The police in Jordan, the FBI and Interpol all believe that the gang was sending the stolen museum goods into Petra and hiding them in the caves.

"It was clever. The caves are a perfect hiding place for stolen property. Jordan has very long desert borders that are hard to control. The local tribesmen have been smuggling goods in and out of Jordan for centuries. And, as I said, the gang has family connections in Jordan.

"Once the stolen goods were in Jordan and hidden in the caves, there was little chance of anyone finding them. The gang used the police who guard the archaeological sites to guard their stolen goods for them.

"So now a lot of people are looking for Ned. The gang is international, and has many connections. Even in places where they don't know anyone, they have enough money to buy help. Interpol told the FBI, so they are looking for Ned in the USA. They have told the Italian police as well."

Virginia and Sarah were very quiet after James finished speaking.

Then Virginia said, "But we can just explain to the police. When they realize it's a big mistake, they will rescue Ned."

James shook his head. "I don't think that will work. If we tell the police where Ned is, they will go and arrest him. They might arrest some gang members as well, but I don't think they will believe Ned's story. We don't even know what Ned's story is. No, we will have to rescue Ned." James took some bread and buttered it.

"How?" asked Virginia.

"I don't know," answered James. "We'll wait until Andy calls us. OK ladies. You need some clothes. You can't go back to Hotel Peschi, and I don't know if this hotel is being watched. I am going to call Senor Manetti and then Luisa. I am sure she would love to bring some clothes for you. Can you make a list?"

Virginia thought the morning was very long. James sat and read a newspaper. He gave Virginia and Sarah books to read. Sarah was happy to read, but Virginia couldn't concentrate.

James ordered sandwiches from room service. Again he told the two women to go into the bedroom before he opened the door.

They ate the sandwiches and drank coffee in silence.

Finally, James' mobile phone rang. It was Andy.

"What have you found out?" James asked Andy.

James listened carefully. Andy talked for about five minutes. James didn't say anything. Then he told Andy he would call him again in about an hour.

"Andy and Antonio have found Ned. They haven't seen him, but there is someone in the tower of Victor's house. They climbed the hill behind the house and watched the window in the tower. They saw the curtain move, and a man looked out. Andy and Antonio were very lucky because there was another man on the hill. He was watching the house too. Luckily they saw him before he saw them, and they were able to hide."

"Are the police watching the house?" asked Sarah.

"No. I don't think the police know where Ned is. Antonio has a cousin who lives in the town. This is very useful. In small towns, everyone sees everything, and they all talk about it. Especially in such a small place, where there are almost no tourists.

"The cousin told Antonio and Andy that a man came to Victor's house about ten days ago. The man is older and he is not Italian. The neighbours think he must have been to the house before. He knew that there was a key hidden behind a rock in the wall. He had no luggage. He went to the supermarket and bought a lot of food and wine. Then he went into the house. The shutters are still locked. A neighbour went to check who was there. But the door was locked, and no one answered. No one has seen the man come out, so they think he is still inside."

"The day after the man locked himself inside Victor's house, four men arrived in two big black cars. They are staying at the hotel. Three of them are from Rome or Milan. Their names are Romero, Luigi and Leon. The other one seems to be an American. They call him Sam. There are always two men watching the house. One man watches the window at the back of the house and the other sits in a car outside the door. They take food and drinks from the hotel and stay there all day and all night. The local people are annoyed because the car blocks the street.

"Remember, Victor's house was built as a small fortress. There are very few windows on the ground floor and those have heavy wooden shutters on them. As you must also remember, the only window without shutters is the one in the tower with the blue lace curtain. It is also the only window at the back of the house."

"This is what I think has happened. The gang found Ned. But they can't get into the house. So they are making sure he can't get out without them catching him."

"But that's good news," said Virginia. "They haven't got Ned!"

"But Virginia," said Sarah. "He can't get out of the house, and if we try to go to Ned, they will see us. Maybe they will shoot at us. I am sure they are the kind of people that have guns."

"Let me think," said James. "I'm sure we can find a way."

11. THE PLAN

Luisa arrived at the hotel with a bag of clothes for Virginia and Sarah.

"Great!" said Virginia and went into the bedroom of the suite to shower and change.

Luisa was excited. "I closed the hotel. Did you call Signor Manetti? Did you explain?" she asked James.

"Yes. I did that. He is travelling back today, and he will reopen the hotel tomorrow. He doesn't think you should stay at the hotel alone, so he said you should stay with your aunt here in Florence tonight. You can go back to the hotel tomorrow."

"You said on the telephone you were Andy's uncle. Where is he?"

"He's busy at the moment, but I am sure you will see him soon." James went to the room that he had used the night before. He came back with his laptop computer, and spent about ten minutes looking at the streets around Victor's house on Google Earth. Then he called someone.

"Guido, my old friend! Yes, this is James. Dinner? I'd love to. But I'm not in Rome. I'm in Florence. When I'm back in Rome, we'll get together. Just now I need some very special information. Can I send you an email?"

Then he took his mobile phone and went out into the corridor to call Andy. Sarah thought this was because he didn't want Luisa to hear his conversation.

Virginia came out of the bedroom and Sarah went to shower and change. James sat and watched his computer screen. An email came.

James seemed very happy with the answer.

When Sarah came back, James was explaining to Virginia and Luisa that he needed to go out for a while.

"I have some things to arrange," he said. "I have a plan. But the plan is going to cost quite a lot of money."

"That's not a problem. I have money," said Virginia. "Even if Ned is an idiot, I want him back."

He repeated the instructions about not opening the door to anyone but him, and went out. Luisa was disappointed.

"This is boring," she said. "No Andy! No shopping!"

"Watch TV," suggested Sarah. "I think things might get more exciting later."

James was gone for about three hours. When he came back, he was carrying some parcels. He wouldn't talk about his plan. He said he would explain when he had finished preparing. Then he went to the other hotel room for about an hour. When he came back he explained the first part of his plan.

"I'll tell you about my ideas for Premilcuore when we get there. First, we have to get out of this hotel. I would be happier if you could stay here, Virginia. But I am worried that if Ned is very frightened, he won't talk to anyone else. I think he needs to see you. Then he will trust us.

"In thirty minutes, the hotel will get a telephone call. The man on the telephone will say that there is a bomb in the hotel. The caller will say it is in room 1047. The staff will go to check. I have left a bag in room 1047 with something that looks like a bomb inside. The hotel will have to tell everyone to leave and call the police. We will already be in the basement car park. While everyone is leaving by the main doors, we will go out through a small side door from the car park. There is a delivery area there for trucks. A van and a driver will be waiting for us. We have to leave in the van before the police arrive and close off the street.

"Luisa. You will come with us. When we are clear of the hotel, we will drop you near a taxi stand. You can take a taxi to your aunt's house."

Luisa was annoyed. "Why do I have to stay with her? It's boring! I thought I would see Andy!"

"I'm sure you'll see him soon," said Sarah. "He will be back at the hotel in two or three days, I hope."

"How did you manage to arrange all of this, James?" Virginia was curious.

James smiled. "A few useful friends and a lot of money!"

They got ready to leave. The two women were wearing jeans, jackets and sports shoes. James took his shopping bags into the bedroom and came out dressed in casual clothes. He was carrying a backpack.

Besides the normal elevators, the hotel had a service elevator for laundry and staff. They took this elevator to the basement of the hotel and waited in a dark corner.

Very soon the fire alarms sounded. They could hear the warning system:

---*Please don't panic. There is no need for alarm, but all guests should leave the hotel as a safety measure. Please use the main stairs or the fire escapes. Do not use the elevators. This is not a practice. Please stay calm.*---

James led the way to the door that opened out into the service area. As he had said, there was a grey van waiting. They climbed into the back of the van, and the driver drove out onto the street. He immediately turned into another narrow street that took them away from the hotel.

They drove through many narrow streets until they finally came back out onto the SS 67. They left Luisa near the Campo di Marte railway station with money to pay for a taxi to her aunt's house.

It took about an hour and a half to get to Premilcuore. The van stopped in a back street, outside a shoe shop. They climbed out, and James led the way into the shop. Even though it was now about 7:00pm, and a Sunday, the shop was open. There was a man in the shop. He didn't speak to them but pointed to a door behind the counter. They found Andy and Antonio in a small storeroom at the back of the shop.

Antonio took them upstairs. There was an apartment above the shop.

"We can use this tonight," he said proudly. "The shoe shop belongs to my cousin. This is his apartment. He will stay at his sister's house. He is happy to help us, but he doesn't want anyone to know."

They sat down in the tiny living room. Antonio brought cheese, salami, bread and wine from the kitchen.

"Now James," said Sarah. "Tell us the plan please!"

"Yes," said Andy. "Antonio and I know some parts, but we don't know all of it."

"Did you talk to someone at the hotel?" asked James.

"Of course," said Antonio. "I found the girl in the kitchen who prepares the food that the men take out with them. It was not difficult at all! The only problem is that the man they call Luigi doesn't drink wine. He only drinks water and she won't be able to put any drugs in that."

"Oh dear," said James. "That could be difficult. Who will be watching from the hill tomorrow?"

"They take turns. Tomorrow, the American, Sam, will be on the hill. He drinks a lot of wine."

"No problem, then. You and Andy can take care of Luigi on the street. The drug will take care of Sam on the hill. And you are sure the girl in the kitchen will do it?"

"Oh, yes. No problem! She says the four men are rude. She doesn't like any of them."

"She wanted a lot of money, though," said Andy. "I had to give Antonio almost all the money you gave me."

"Never mind that," said James. He took a small envelope from his pocket and gave it to Antonio.

"I got this from a pharmacy in Florence. If she puts it in their wine, they should fall asleep within a few minutes of drinking it. You had better take it to her tonight after we finish talking about the plan.

"Now listen, everyone. My plan depends on the fact that there must be another way into the house. When the house was built, it was intended to protect the family in times of war. That is why it is so strong. But think about Ned's situation. His enemies can't get in, but he can't get out. He is a prisoner. I was sure the people who built the house thought of this. There must be a second door or hidden entrance. So I asked my friend Guido. He agreed. He said the most common hidden access in houses of that type was a tunnel. It would be under the house in the basement. Does Victor's house have a basement, Virginia?"

"Oh, yes," answered Virginia. "Victor stored wine in it. But it's empty now."

"I looked on Google Earth and I think I know where the entrance to the tunnel is. There is a small building on the hill behind the house. I am sure it is in there. The problem is that the men who watch the house sit in front of it. But Antonio has solved that problem. Now this is what we are going to do."

James talked for about twenty minutes. "Is everyone happy?" he asked.

Everyone nodded. Antonio would deliver the sleeping drug to the hotel kitchen. He was going to stay with his cousins.

The three men and two women drank some wine and went over the plans again.

Virginia yawned. "I am sorry," she said. "I feel very sleepy. I haven't been sleeping well. Now that we have a plan and I might see Ned tomorrow, I am much more relaxed."

"Well I think we all need to get some sleep. I know I do," said James. "I didn't get much sleep on either Friday night or last night. Tomorrow will be a busy day."

Antonio went away with the envelope and everyone else tried to sleep. Sarah and Virginia were in the only bedroom. James and Andy lay down on the floor of the living room.

Why couldn't we stay in a hotel like normal people? Andy asked himself. *At least I would have a bed.* He answered the question for himself. *There is only one hotel. And the gangsters are staying there.*

12. THE RESCUE

At 7:00 the next morning, the American gangster, Sam Black, went down to the kitchen in the hotel to collect the bags of food Luigi had ordered for them. Sam was getting bored with cheese, salami and bread. But it seemed the kitchen had no imagination. If you asked for picnic food, they gave you cheese, salami and bread. Sam was bored with watching the house too. He was getting a lot of money for this job, but it wasn't enough.

Boring food and boring work, he thought. *I don't think that guy will ever come out. They should pay me more just to stay awake. And it's my turn on the hill today. I hope it doesn't rain.*

Usually Luigi collected the picnic meals from the kitchen, but he was in a bad mood today. Sam thought that Luigi was bored too. Then Sam cheered up. At least there would be wine. And he would ask for two bottles today.

Luigi was waiting with the car outside the hotel. They didn't speak as they drove to Victor's house. There was a car parked outside the door. It blocked the narrow street. Luigi stopped behind the car. Luigi and Sam went to talk to the driver.

"Any action, Leon?" asked Luigi.

"Nothing," answered Leon. Sam walked 200m down the road and then climbed some steep steps that led to a small park on the hill. From there he walked across the hill to the small stone building where Romero was sitting.

"Anything happen?" Sam asked Romero.

Romero yawned. "Nothing. I'm cold. Have a good day!"

Romero walked away down the hill to where Leon was waiting for him. Sam saw the car drive away back towards the hotel. He sat down and picked up the binoculars. The man in the tower didn't appear very early. It was usually about 10:00 or 11:00 before he started peeping out from behind the curtain. Sam thought about a gun. It would be so easy to shoot the guy. He wasn't far away. But they had been told to keep him alive. The boss wanted information.

Sam was the man who had spoken to Sarah and Virginia on the telephone. It had been easy. They had almost caught Ned in Florence, but Romero had fallen over on the stairs. The guy had heard them. When they finally got into the room, they found that Ned had escaped out the window. But he had left everything behind. His mobile phone and a map with Premilcuore marked in pencil. What an idiot!

Of course he had told Virginia that they would kill Ned. He had offered the exchange of the dagger for Ned. But the boss wanted the dagger and he planned to keep Ned. A second plan was to snatch the wife, and then tell Ned they would kill her if he didn't come out. But the wife seemed to be a bit smarter than her husband. The idiots who were watching that little hotel where she was staying had followed her and her friend to Florence. Then they had lost them. Perhaps that friend of hers, the one with the strange accent, was the smart one. Anyway, they had lost the wife and maybe the dagger. Now it was even more important to watch the tower.

Down in the town, the shoe shop opened as usual at 9:00am. Upstairs in the apartment, the rescue team was eating breakfast.

"There's no need to hurry," said James. "We can't do anything until Sam is asleep. He probably won't eat and drink anything until lunchtime. It will take us about an hour and a half to walk around the hill and approach it from the other side. So if we leave here at ten o' clock, it should be fine."

Just as they were leaving the apartment, James handed Sarah a handgun.

"I hope you don't have to use this," he said. "But if anything goes wrong…"

Sarah nodded without saying anything. She took the gun and checked it, then stuck it in the waistband of her jeans under her jacket.

Andy was annoyed. "Where's my gun?" he asked.

"You and Antonio will be on the street," James replied. "I don't think there will be any reason for shooting on the street. And do you know how to use a gun?"

Of course Andy didn't know how to use a gun, but he was still annoyed.

"Do you have a gun?" he asked.

"Yes. And I have a rifle. Now can we leave, please?"

James, Virginia and Sarah walked through the back streets of the town. It took a long time. They walked to the far end of the town and climbed the hill behind Victor's house from the opposite side. At the top of the hill, they could look down on the little stone building where Sam was watching. Then, very quietly, they went down the hill until they were just behind the building.

"We'll have to wait," said James. "We don't know when he'll drink the wine. Or how much he'll drink. We can't move until he's asleep."

By noon, Sam was hungry and thirsty. He opened a bottle of wine. He drank some. It didn't taste as good as usual. It was a different type of wine. This one had a screw cap not a cork. Perhaps he would have water instead.

Water! he thought. *I left all the water in the car with Luigi! I'll have to drink the wine.* He drank more wine and ate some cheese and bread.

Then, very slowly he fell sideways. He was asleep.

James slid around the side of the building. He had a gun in his hand. Very soon, he came back. He put the gun away.

"He's asleep. Come on."

Sam was lying in front of the building. "He shouldn't wake up for at least an hour," said James. "Those knock-out drugs are very effective."

The two women followed James around to the front of the building. Virginia looked up at the tower. *Ned's there,* she thought. *If everything goes well, I'll see him soon.*

The building had a wide opening, but no door or windows. The walls were made of stone but the floor was earth. There was some firewood stacked against the walls. They stepped over Sam and went in. James took two large torches from his backpack.

"We have to find the entrance to the tunnel. It will be hidden. It might take us a long time."

Sarah and James shone the torches on the walls and floor. Virginia pointed to the floor in one corner. "There's something different there."

James looked. "Yes, the level is different." He took a small collapsible shovel from his backpack and assembled it. He started digging and scraping the earth in the corner. Very soon a square stone appeared. Sarah and Virginia picked up pieces of firewood and helped scrape the earth away.

When the edges of the stone were clear, James pushed the edge of the shovel under the stone. It was heavy, but they finally lifted the stone. There were stone steps going down into the darkness. "Pass me a torch, will you please?" asked James.

Sarah handed him a torch. He climbed down the steps. At the bottom of the steps he looked up at them.

"I'm going to check. Sarah, the rifle's in my backpack. Go outside and watch. Take the rifle."

"What's she supposed to do if anyone comes?" asked Virginia.

"If they're local people, talk to them. If it's one of the men from the hotel, shoot him. Try not to kill anyone. Aim for the leg."

Then he disappeared.

Sarah took the rifle, loaded it and went outside.

Virginia lay on the floor and stared down the steps.

It was about twenty minutes before James came back.

"It's OK. The tunnel is in good condition. The entrance to the wine cellar is clear. I was worried it might be blocked," he told Virginia.

He went to the door and spoke to Sarah. "It will take you about ten minutes to get into the house. Call me as soon as you're in the wine cellar, then I'll call Andy."

"Ned's up and moving around," Sarah told him. "I saw the curtain move. He's watching."

"Virginia. Come out here, please," James ordered. Virginia came out.

"Ned is watching us. Come and wave to him. Try to show him that you are not our prisoner."

Virginia came out and waved towards the window with the blue lace curtain. She couldn't see Ned but the curtain seemed to move.

"OK. Time to go."

Sarah handed the rifle to James. James gave Sarah his torch. Virginia went back inside.

Sarah turned to follow her. "Wait!" said James.

Sarah looked at him. He put out his hand and touched her face. "Be careful."

Sarah smiled and put her hand over his. "I will be."

Then she was gone.

Ten minutes later, Sarah called James. "We're in the basement. I think I can hear Ned moving around just above us. So he might be on the first floor."

"Be careful. He's been alone and scared for days. We don't know what he might do if he thinks he is being attacked, or if he thinks Virginia is in danger. It's time for me to call Andy."

James called Andy. "Now!" he said.

Antonio and Andy had been waiting with Antonio's motorbike further down the street.

They climbed onto the bike and raced up the street towards Luigi's car. Andy was waving a wine bottle and shouting.

"Have a drink with us! Come on. My friend is getting married! Drink, drink!"

The bike stopped next to the car. Andy banged on the window with his wine bottle. "Drink! Drink!"

Luigi told Andy and Antonio to go away. They didn't seem to hear him. He tried to get out of the car, but the motorbike was blocking the door.

Just then a woman appeared pushing a baby carriage, she walked past the other side of the car and started shouting too.

"Stop that noise! It's waking the baby!"

Luigi moved across and tried to get out the passenger door but the baby carriage was blocking the way. Other people arrived and stood around the car. Everyone was shouting.

"You're blocking the road! Stop the noise! You'll wake the baby! Drink! Drink!"

There were now about twenty people shouting. They stood very close to the car. Luigi couldn't see out of the car windows. He didn't see the door to Victor's house open and three people come out. Andy was still banging on the window with the wine bottle, but Antonio was not there. The man who came out of the house climbed onto the back of Antonio's motorbike and they rode away. The two women from the house were walking down the street. Finally, the noise stopped and everyone disappeared. They didn't go very far. At the bottom of the street, the woman with the baby carriage was taking bottles of wine out of the carriage and was serving drinks. Virginia was handing out money and thanking everyone.

Luigi was finally alone again. *Crazy people!* he thought. He opened a bottle of water and his bag of food. He watched the door of the house.

On the hill, Sam was waking up. He had a headache and felt bad. *I must have had too much wine,* he thought. *I don't think that wine is very good. I'll ask for the normal wine tomorrow. And I'll have some water too.*

13. NED'S STORY

The van that James had hired was waiting outside the shoe shop. Virginia gave Antonio's cousin some money and climbed into the back of the van. Ned was there.

"Oh, Ned! Thank God you're safe!"

Antonio was talking to James. "Time for me to go! Tell me next time you need some help. I've never had so much fun!"

He roared away on his motorbike.

Andy, James and Sarah got into the van too and they drove away.

As the van driver drove them back to Hotel Peschi, Ned explained his part of the story.

"I was searching the caves at Petra. The other archaeologists were working on the buildings of the city. But I had a feeling the caves might be very important. I found signs that the Crusaders had used them. I thought the Crusaders might have hidden treasure there."

"Ned! That's just a story. That Indiana Jones movie was about finding treasure at Petra!" Virginia shook her head.

"No! Think about it! The Indiana Jones story was based on a legend. But many legends are based on truth. Indiana Jones found the Egyptian Pharaoh's treasure in a tomb. I was looking for Crusader treasure. Gold stolen from the Saracens, and buried in a cave. It's not the same thing!

"I found some signs that my ideas were correct. I knew I could make a great discovery. I wanted to be famous. My guide was always with me. Then one day he had a toothache. He stayed at the bottom of the cliff and I was alone. I took my chance. There was one area my guide refused to go. He said the caves were dangerous there. He wasn't with me, so I took a risk and went there alone.

"I didn't find anything connected with the Crusaders. But I did go into a cave that was filled with wooden boxes. I opened some. There were paintings, statues and mummies. I realised that someone was hiding things in the cave. I guessed my guide knew about it. But I had no idea who was hiding things. I took the smallest thing I could find. I took the dagger. I thought it would be easy to hide and easy to carry. I planned to go to the police.

"I left the cave and went back to my guide. But he wasn't there. A worker told me that the guide had run away. Then he said that the police were there and they were looking for me and looking for my guide.

"I panicked. I went back to my hotel and checked out. I wanted to get out of the Middle East. I went to the airport. There was a flight to Cairo. I took it. In Cairo I started thinking about the dagger. I knew it was European, not Arabic. It looked about 16th or 17th century.

"I checked on the Internet. I found a professor at a university in Florence. He is an expert on weapons. I went to Florence and I showed him a photograph of the dagger. He told me what it was, and that it had been stolen. I decided to take it to the American Embassy in Rome. I thought I could explain to the Embassy staff and they could help me explain to the police. But then I realized I was being followed. I didn't know who it was. I guess the professor must have told someone about me, and about the dagger. I mailed the dagger to Virginia and went to the airport. The same men were at the airport. I couldn't get on a plane to Rome. I went back to the hotel and called Sarah. Then I heard someone on the stairs. I climbed out the window with my wallet and nothing else. I got to Premilcuore and I thought I was safe. Then the same four men arrived. I had left the map with the town marked in my hotel room. The rest you know. I did all the wrong things. I feel stupid."

"Never mind, Ned." Virginia was holding his hand. "I've given the dagger to James and he has a friend in Interpol. You don't have to think about it anymore. The Italian police will pick up the men in Premilcuore. We'll go to Hotel Peschi and have a lovely dinner with the Manettis."

They arrived at the hotel in the middle of the afternoon. Luisa threw herself into Andy's arms. "I have been so worried. How could

The Blue Lace Curtain

your uncle ask you to help in something so dangerous?"

Andy was delighted. "Well, I enjoyed it," he said. "But I missed you!"

"Luisa" said Signora Manetti. "Let go of that young man and come with me. We have a feast to cook!"

"Yes, a celebration," smiled Signor Manetti. "It's so good to see you again, my dear friend James. It's been too long since we drank wine together. Now you come back here with your friends and a story to tell us. I want to hear everything."

Signora Manetti disappeared to the kitchen taking Luisa with her. Everyone else showered and changed.

Signor Manetti was serving drinks to everyone in the dining room when Ned reappeared. He looked like a different person, wearing clothes borrowed from Andy. He had been wearing the clothes he escaped from Florence in for almost two weeks. He sat next to Virginia and held her hand. "I was thinking I might never see you again. I promise I will never get into so much trouble again."

"You won't be able to," laughed Virginia. "I'm not going to let you go away without me."

It was a wonderful dinner. The Manettis and Luisa joined them at the big round table in the centre of the dining room. Everyone talked and laughed. Ned heard what had happened while he was trapped in Victor's house. The Manettis and Luisa heard the whole story for the first time.

Andy was still puzzled about one thing.

"Sarah," he said. "I have just one question."

"Yes?" said Sarah.

"How do you know how to use a handgun and a rifle?"

"I grew up in Scotland. My father had a lot of land. He had a farm, fishing rivers and some small forests. We call them estates. We lived in the highlands so we used to hunt deer. That's why I can use a rifle."

"And the handgun?"

"My father collected small guns. He taught me to shoot with a handgun when I was about ten."

Andy looked at James. "And you knew all of this?" he asked.

James smiled at Sarah. "Well, forty years ago, we were very good friends."

By 9:00pm everyone was tired. Andy was helping Luisa wash

dishes in the kitchen. The Manettis said goodnight and went to their apartment above the kitchen. Virginia and Ned went to their room. Only Sarah and James were left at the table. James smiled at Sarah. "Come out onto the terrace, we need to talk."

"I'll get my coat," said Sarah.

When she joined James on the terrace, he was standing looking out over the trees. She stood next to him and they didn't speak for several minutes.

Then James said, "I can't believe that I am here with you. It's something I thought could never happen."

"In the beginning, I thought you were dead," said Sarah. "When you left Paris so suddenly, and then never contacted me, I thought you must have died. Even if you didn't want to see me, I thought you would send a letter or telephone to explain. But there was nothing."

"I know. I hated it. It's been forty years, so I can talk about it now, if you want to listen. I will understand if you don't."

"Tell me," Sarah spoke quietly.

"When I was in my last year of university in England, I was offered a job with a British intelligence agency. I was an unusual student. My father was a doctor. He specialised in treating Asian diseases. By the time I went to boarding school in England when I was twelve, I had lived for four years in Cambodia and five years in China. I spoke both languages quite well. Then at university I studied Arabic. They thought I would be useful because I had such an unusual combination of languages. Anyway, I accepted the job. They suggested I spent some more time at university, studying European languages, so that's why I went to the Sorbonne.

"I was supposed to start work in London as a translator, when I finished my courses in Paris. Then I met you. I fell in love with you. Even though I was only hired as a translator, I wasn't allowed to tell anyone who I was going to work for. I was supposed to lie and say I was working for an insurance company. But I couldn't lie to you. I couldn't tell you the truth either.

"I had decided to ask you to marry me. If you said 'yes', I was going to break the rules and tell you about my job. Then suddenly I was contacted and told to go to England immediately. You and Virginia had gone sailing. I couldn't contact you. I went to London, and twenty-four hours later I was in Cambodia. Some journalists had been kidnapped. The British believed they had been taken by the

Khmer Rouge to Lumphat. I was sent to gather information, because I had lived in Lumphat when I was a child. A family who used to work for my father took me in and hid me.

"In London, they had said I would be in Cambodia for ten days to three weeks. They were wrong. Conditions changed very suddenly. I couldn't leave Cambodia. I was trapped in Lumphat for eleven months. Every day I was hiding in that place, and wondering if I would be captured, I thought of you. When I got back, I went to look for you. I found out you had married. I could understand if you didn't want to see me, but I was surprised you married so quickly. I thought perhaps you hadn't loved me. So, I never tried to write to you or call you."

"It wasn't like that, James. Please try to understand. I thought you were dead. I was so unhappy. I didn't finish my course at the Sorbonne. I went home to Scotland. My father was very ill. He was dying of cancer. I needed help to run the estate, so I married a friend of my family's. He was twelve years older than me. In the beginning he was very kind to me. My father died soon after we married. Then fifteen years ago, my husband died. I sold the estate and moved to my mother's old family home. It is near Oban. I've been there ever since. I knew you were still alive because about twenty years ago, I saw your name and your photograph in the international section of the newspaper."

"And now, Sarah. This lucky chance has brought us together. Virginia and Ned are leaving tomorrow. But will you stay? I know we can't go back forty years. But maybe we can go forward. I would like to spend some time with you."

"No James. Not now. I want to go back to Scotland and think about everything. Please give me some time."

"Can I email you? Can I call you?"

"Of course," Sarah smiled.

"And come and visit you?"

"Perhaps. Let's wait and see what happens."

I Talk You Talk Press

THANK YOU

Thank you for reading The Blue Lace Curtain. (Word count: 15,627) If you enjoyed this story, you might also like End House, Book 2 in the Old Secrets - Modern Mysteries Series.

If you would like to read more graded readers, please visit our website http://www.italkyoutalk.com

Other Level 4 graded readers include
Chi-obaa and Friends
Chi-obaa and Her Town
End House (Old Secrets – Modern Mysteries Book 2)
On the Run (Old Secrets – Modern Mysteries Book 3)
The Blue Lace Curtain (Old Secrets – Modern Mysteries Book 1)
The Witches of Nakashige
Vanished Away

ABOUT THE AUTHOR

I Talk You Talk Press is a Japan-based publisher of language textbooks, graded readers and language learning/teaching resources.

Our team is made up of highly experienced language teachers and translators, who have all studied at least one additional language to an advanced level.

This experience enables us to design our materials from the perspective of both the teacher and the learner. We consult with both teachers and language learners when designing our textbooks and graded readers, and test our materials extensively in the classroom before publication.

We are a fast-growing press, and currently publish graded readers for learners of English. We publish new graded readers monthly.

www.ingramcontent.com/pod-product-compliance
Lightning Source LLC
Chambersburg PA
CBHW022342040426
42449CB00006B/685